Lizard

for
Lisl/Liesl
1904–1941


and for
Andreas, Arielle, Benjamin, Julius, Raquel

Lizard means I
don't speak your
language. She means
I don't share your
brain. She learns with
her scan. Negotiates
with tail and jaw.
Her response is
nuanced. But your
grid trances her,
hunger saps, leash
abrades. Your gaze
a promise you
can't keep

Sometimes she
collaborates.
Sometimes self-
propagates. Progeny
true replicas. Study
any one of them. Each
mirrors her cell. Her
breath. Her deliberate
gait. Her fracture line.
Her frictional adhesion.
Her prehistoric.
Her salivate.
Her scale

10

A bad translation
has Lizard cutting
off her tail to spite
her fate. But she
grows a new one.
Steers with it.
Stores fat against
the slim days.
Replaceable
parts help L stay
cutting edge. She's
working on her
head. Only her
belly is famously
hers and can be
stroked. She'll turn
over

When danger's
near she pours
her flesh into
purchased beige,
becomes a
dish too ugly
to taste. Out
of harm's way
she sloughs pale
cells, radiance
gazes out like a
necklace everyone
wears

She rests lightly
awaiting
messengers.
Drifts off to
wake famished.
But feeding's a
chore to a groggy
girl. She sprawls
in a cloud of bad
breath wanting to
warm the day,
warm to the day,
day isn't hers, it
borrows

Ovo-, vivi-,
ovoviviparous,
she grips sounds
with her fused
toes

She says no,
yes, someone
bites her neck
and she produces

Her neck heals
completely, she
falls fifty feet

Falls for color

One eye on making

She rests, pulsing,
skin wishbone
dry. Part of you
wishes to touch her

We used to say,
cold blooded. Now
we know, Lizard's
no bitch. She
regulates. Revises
her heat to match
the universe. Seeks

agreement

We used to think,
tolerates extremes.
Lizard expires at
our limit. But walks
right up to that
edge. Pleasure a
single step from
not here

Questions you
might have: Why
is her blood clear,
poison slow, her
God borrowed?
Does a mate support?
Does she bake? Do
her eggs crack?                    17

Lizard bakes
on asphalt. A
car might crush
or maim her. Dear
God, she writes,
why have I lost
capacity, learned

pain? Where are
my offspring?
Do you see them
sprinkled in the
world? Do you
see my end? My
poison poor defense,
my blood clear
offense. My
recourse speed
and hide

Eight reasons
to change color,
emotion weather
etc. Not a quiz,
she says. And
only sometimes
do I blend to
background                              19

Wants to talk
strategy. Confined
how will you move
backward and
forth, she wants
to be asked. How
far will you see
your stranger

Knows frightened
and magical tricks.
Been known to
leave you holding
her startled skin

My kind's on
the exit list says
Lizard. I'll miss
every bird, look,
high-branched nap.
No prehensile tail
will coil. No eye
swivel solo

She grapples
with her conditions.
Given fewer
colors, rushed
and bitten. Love
is not discussed.
She climbs into
20        her corners. A
little fact: Lizard
can produce ideas
immaculate. Her
spitting image.
Knowing girls
improves the pool

Lizard have you
been writing in bed?

Don't force courtesy
on Lizard

She writes at night,
her scales
absorb the dark

Two anecdotes:

Someone eating tacos
tells Lizard things
she already knows

Lizard gets offered
the role of virgin.
I can do this,
she tells herself

Someone at a party
thought she said
literature. I did,
she says. I might
as well have

It's like not/knot,
sock/sock,
look up/look up.
Lizard's very earrings
shiver feelings

She befriends
her obstacles—
eagle, sun, neck-
biting mate. Carves
a poem from every
gesture: dig, roll,
tap, dash, curl.

Freeze and thaw
are Lizard's fridge
magnets. Give, her
motive force. Keep,
nothing she knows.
Leave, a day's work

When her tongue
whips prey, your
own heart clenches

I eat my sister. No
one cares because
we're not pronouns,
says Lizard. We're
not names. I'm not
Lizard and this is
not a magic act. This
is real, tongue so
long and muscular,
toes scaling verticals,
third eye parietal

She flops on a
strange bed under
an accusing moon.
L's been charged with:

obstinacy (primordial)

sluttishness (mates multiply)                    25

prudery (she skitters away)

repulsiveness (scales)

necrophilia (garden of bone)

the Fall (guilt by association)

greed (butterfly wings crushed
between jaws)

jealousy, disrespect for beauty (destroys
her lovely sister)

Mostly eats the living.
On account of her
eyes. They see what
moves. She stalks
the world nude, I
want to say reveals
the world's nudity.
Want to say, we're
all that emperor.
That lonely thing
with mirrors

L, I made you
that way. Nothing
you can do.
Sluggish at dawn,
brutal at noon.
Where are you?
Where I dreamed
you, in the rickety
city up multiple
flights peeking at
neighbors in their
kitchens. They'll
be your dance
to death partners.
Acquaint yourself

Farmers dig deep
placing seedlings
to sprout in time.
So Lizard. Rug
makers dream
baroque patterns.
So Lizard. Scholars
hang Do Not
Disturb from
the knob. See
Lizard. Singers
croon of hap-
hazard encounters.
Sigh Lizard

Lizard is wild
and Lizard is
you. Remember
this standing,
sitting, gripping
a lid to twist. Erase
the last word,
replace it, you
are her. Savor
knowing location.
You are here in
everymap

Can't get anything
done—first condition
—till she's wrong
enough. Warm I
mean. Rotates as if
on a spit. Suddenly
too much heat and
she slips under sand.
Names the day
precarious like a
daughter

Questions you might
have: Will a lizard
drink? Do parasites
creep under her skin?
Do you know her
dose? Will she
tolerate a triangle?
Are hyacinths
preferred? Why
does she exhibit
her stay away coat
this morning?

When you read
about Lizard you
may feel bliss.
That's her deep
moment rubbing
off on you. Lizard's
a teenager hungry
and perfect, an
elder bemused by
stingers. She thanks
each one in their
own tongue. Her
means world …
what did you just
forget, remember?
L touches every fact
and you touch L

Lizard stalks
images so vivid
they cut. A
friend in fuschia
saying let's try
a new process.
(Lizard's wearing
orange, it
complements her
natural green.)
We'll argue. (It's
more elaborate but
that's the gist.) It
will make our ideas
better.
        I like the
streaks on you,
your toned
commitment

I should know
more. Should I
count her, make
a mark. Tell
over drinks. She
scurried into
underbrush. Yea
long. Thus colored.
Horn occipital.
As if skin listens.
Later you muse on
memory's nature

Study the other,
ask the librarian
to carry it

L takes pleasure
in worship places.
Stone alcove, cool
tile. Silent as a
devotee—when
she shouts, it's raw
notes. Swallows
butterflies, stunning
wings. Advises
monks on famous
honey

Sometimes L
forces herself
to watch the
monster movie.
Starring her, the
evil monster. Old
story. Look at
me, sunning.
Medieval dragon
if you say so. But
hero too, in
fabulist mail.
Virgin, hewn
jewel

Sometimes she sleeps
with her street clothes
on. Sometimes
she walks in
her intimates

Elliptical slit
allows for light
—innuendo—
a well placed
stroke, a manner
of lifting, sweat
forms, sweet
gathers and now
what—she clears
her throat

—Throw "she"
in there and Lizard
immediately thinks it's
her

I'll trade you dreams
for poems says L.
Fork over then.
She pours dreams*
into hungry sky
mouth. Now send
that rain says L.
As promised                          41

*It's mostly the wind
carrying me, she
shouts down to the
businessmen. See
look I'm falling as
we speak. But it's
not the wind, she's
not falling, she
skims garden walls
and then what

L's being handed
a made thing
the story of L

full of trails
and false
origins

I wear the stay away
coat till I've written
down my dreams.
There are coats for
any occasion. Coat
of arms, sugar coat.
Parasitic load may
be managed, given
other factors. Hyacinth,
yes, but nasturtium
too, and dandelion,
and the rose. Hydration
is key and never
standing. Only in
motion is water to me

Holds pen above
page waiting. Arm
goes numb, mind
flops, hallucinating
rivers, whitewater but
they're damming that
one aren't they? I saw
the documentary. I'll
put my hand on an
anxious shoulder and
say *breathe three times*

I've traded cheap
thrills for the bliss
discipline. You're
my regimen

L requires just-
right conditions.
Did you bargain
it? Entertaining
on a date, now
you're saddled
with her list. Light,
heart, diet. She's no
trick. Kept is kept
alive

Questions you may
have: How does a
lizard feel pain?
Does she remember
five minutes ago?
Did you push your
luck with her? Is
she the girl across
a crowded room?
Does she point like
an arrow, audition,
listen, soak?

Lizard's a slapstick
actor. Her timing's
no timing, her
grace is no grace.
She's cutest when
she doesn't know
her name. So how
are you, vertiginous,
you've been waiting
for a lizard to topple
you, now it happens,
now go build a frame
for the raw moment

She has landed.
She's in the seat
of bite. She's
dreaming tongues and
thunder. Sound is
what binds her.
*Inscrutable,* she
whispers, *why*
*would I want that*
*word? Blues hard*
*enough,* she croons.
All night trades
appetites, all day
seeks cover. Drinks
in the happy hour

I forgot poems for
a reading. I had one,
filled with typos.
Luckily the hostess
had a copy of the
Lizard manuscript.
Do you like it, a
question I never
ask. She laughed.
I'd been parking
the cars of my
elders. So it goes
in the dream of
Lizard

Once Lizard's done
what she can—birth
control, death control
—she listens—to
ice breaking off
the mass, growth
smothering a
reef. Whatever
she attends to she
becomes—a word
on the page till
the book is lost,
a shape in the
clouds till the
hurricane. She
blends into bark
while arsonists
brood, subject
of talk till dessert
is served

The lights go out.
You pitch in the dark.
You dream and wake
and think of Lizard

She's in the dirt.
In front of our
house I spot her.
I want listening
to write the poem,
Lizard escapes my
grasp every time.
Metaphorically. Say
L lives nearby
outside wild. I'm
lazy watching,
knowing little. She
can't not stand my
presence. Her sudden
form defines the zero
point I so adore

What about her mind,
her friend, her thirst?
What limbs has she
perched on? What
fences, what fruit,
what stillborns on
what beds? What
does a lizard mean
when she says I,
my, me? How does
a lizard sing?

At her best
gestural. And
a little lost

The secret wants
to be told. Why
doesn't she have the
secret man in the third
row tell, he squeals,
hand up—pick me.
By all means says L.
But he just reveals his
cover, and just to the
secret listeners.
They listen politely,
praying he doesn't
dominate the evening
in which their secret
hearts pound

55

She flies, functionally
speaking. Ribs
arcing she sails
unerring to the next
point

Drop my guard
unless threatened.
Drop my eggs in
promising locations.
Keep my tail if
possible. Be profligate
with color. Variegated
by design. Nod rhythm.
Scream my glad notes

Tail. Cell. Femoral pore.

Ventricle. Vertibra.

Cloaca. Tympana

It's the hour to
be coaxed from
my hole with licks
and rubs, lie with
you in the inches
and discipline of
time, in the silence
of our chemical
embrace, do it
again intelligent
times, patiently
helping nothing
tumble into some-
thing. My worries
begin now. I'll be
officer of the
unseen for the
duration and I
should feel thanks.
You clamp to
disable my bite.
Yours keeps the
show going, mine
just hurts

seeing: she licks her lids
snake: interior landscapes resemble
asphalt: mistaken for life-giving warmth of rock
she never: waits or cries
wait: it's you who wait and when you wait you
        are most like Lizard

Parasites burrow
under your skin, into
your gut, gorge
to enlarge. Where
they creep you bulge
inelegantly, ooze
infection. Are you

wise to tolerate, do
you have enough,
does saying no
buck nature? You
don't blame beings
designed to leech.
Everyone's born
with a strategy. And
then we execute

You means live
through things.
When you stop
the pronouns
explode

I said blinking, you
sat blinking but in
slow motion

I said jump and
you said OK but
got distracted

I said cost x cents
at the market. And
lived x days. And
those should have been
two easy A's

I said define
manipulate and you
rubbed your digit
around on a hard
surface, groggy
with desire to get
out

Is a lizard nature?
Does she know
providence? Was
she ever stitched?
Do darlings claim
her? Does she
sweat? Dream?
Curl in? Levitate?

Her defenders:
"Millennia, plethora,
tongue long as a mile"

"Don't scare her or
pick her up by the tail"

Delicate mention of
mass destruction tucked
just before index

"Canary. She's down
in that mine. That's why
you should care"

Have you had enough
grief? There's more.
When all is quiet
it forms in words
as simple as a cup.
It clings to her like
lotion, invisible
silken. The cup is
cracked and the
lotion stings, thoughts
form a hood and
finally she falls
asleep to dream of
impossible cakes and
conductors on tiptoe
putting out fires
before the place
burns down

Lost in the terrain
of her skin up
close. Plateaus
and ravines. Far
enough into the
moment you're
timeless. Thanks
to a shakeup or
lots of practice

Some say L is
stupid. She tastes
her information.
Some have stopped
having that
conversation. She
stares into the sun
with her third eye.
Documentary

Does not levitate.
Lifts herself in
sections. Dreams
of prodigious
multiples. Sits in
the Lost and Found.
Fills out a form and
takes herself home

O divine incident/study/motion,
where to go from here?

There is a fire, there
are dollars performed,
there is a crowd
of onlookers expecting

You don't know. And
that's because you
came to this out of
deep sleep, like the
rest of us. You give
and sink back,
give and sink back

Oviposited. You must
be resting now. And
we're waiting, in our
leathery skins

She becomes a pool,
a cake, dried blood, a
reticent football star,
a go getter childhood
friend

Sometimes she has to
stuff her ears, cover
her eyes to know
less

Sometimes she sleeps
on a hard bed to
eke out more

A pen snakes away
like it's not related

But pens are her
siblings or long
lost cousins leaving
a twitching tail

She knows a lot
like what was in
the novelist's head
when he described
those bodies, the
red haired pouty
one, exposed clavicle,

eyes set wide, the
one whose shoulders
hunch diminishing
height

She knows the
novelist, his 9,000
ideas through which
bodies slip

*What is a normal*
*pre-born Jane?*
*Isn't this place*
*open Sundays?*
*What's the code?*
*What's salvageable?*

So there you lie
in that town now
Lizard, the light
burning through
your closed lids
like a mother
phoning her way
past the outgoing
message

I've heard our name
isn't short
for anything

All the words in
this poem rebel
because Lizard
I'm unimagining
you. A guttural
hope would have
to seduce me now,
a stage whisper

I know what a gun
can do, a hand. My
heart beats against
its walls
                What are
you doing today?
Love is love and
praise my inabilities

The next lines read
we coexisted for
a time. You are
a parent a sibling
of mine. A passing
tryst, a grabbed
wrist

The great happiness
of a lizard
assembling reality
one scale at a time
one pulse

rest on a railing
take up vision's
invitation
flick your tongue
on memory
send it
upward

sound is a
whatever waterfall
bringing a wealth
of zeroes

you borrow the
classiest weather
stormy grays

bones and blood
contemplate
motion's miracle

you are the hour's
favorite acolyte

electric even

She wears five
bows and a dream
flag, swaggers out
to the humid dangers,
bumped she lashes,
topples, starts over

Mostly we're not
original wrote the
poet and L agrees.
Shares her gait,
her tactic. Doesn't
stake; she contributes.
Iterates. Accepts
her status as a
fabulous specimen.
Nevertheless it
must be said
Lizard's inspired.
She breathes. And
registers the slightest
shift in weather

## About the Author

Sarah Rosenthal is the author of *Manhatten* (Spuyten Duyvil, 2009) as well as several chapbooks including *Estelle Meaning Star* (above/ground, 2014), *disperse* (Dusie, 2014), *The Animal* (in collaboration with artist Amy Fung-yi Lee, Dusie, 2011), *How I Wrote This Story* (Margin to Margin, 2001), *sitings* (a+bend, 2000), and *not-chicago* (Melodeon, 1998). She edited *A Community Writing Itself: Conversations with Vanguard Poets of the Bay Area* (Dalkey Archive, 2010). Her poetry has appeared in journals such as *Eleven Eleven, Sidebrow, Zen Monster, Otoliths, eccolinguistics, textsound,* and *Little Red Leaves,* and is anthologized in *Kindergarde: Avant-garde Poems, Plays, and Stories for Children* (Black Radish, 2013), *Building is a Process / Light is an Element: essays and excursions for Myung Mi Kim* (P-Queue, 2008), *Bay Poetics* (Faux, 2006), *The Other Side of the Postcard* (City Lights, 2004), and *hinge* (Crack, 2002). Her essays and interviews have appeared in journals such as *Jacket, Denver Quarterly, Rain Taxi, New American Writing,* and *How2.* She is the recipient of the Leo Litwak Fiction Award, a Creative Capacity Innovation Grant, a San Francisco Education Fund Grant, and grant-supported writing residencies at Vermont Studio Center, Soul Mountain, and Ragdale. From 2009–2011 she was an Affiliate Artist at Headlands Center for the Arts. She is a Life & Professional Coach and serves on the California Book Awards poetry jury.

## About CHAX

Founded in 1984 in Tucson, Arizona, Chax has published nearly 200 books in a variety of formats, including hand printed letterpress books and chapbooks, hybrid chapbooks, book arts editions, and trade paperback editions such as the book you are holding. In August 2014 Chax moved to Victoria, Texas, and is presently located in the University of Houston Victoria Center for the Arts, which has generously supported the publication of *Lizard*, which has also received support from many friends of the press. Chax is an independent 501(c)(3) organization which depends on support from various government and private funders, and, primarily, from individual donors and readers.

Recent and current books-in-progress include *The Complete Light Poems,* by Jackson Mac Low, *Life-list,* by Jessica Smith, *Andalusia,* by Susan Thackrey, *Diesel Hand,* by Nico Vassilakis, *Dark Ladies,* by Steve McCaffery, *The Collected Poems of Gil Ott, An Intermittent Music,* by Ted Pearson, *Limerence,* by Saba Razvi, and several other books to come.

You may find CHAX online at *http://chax.org*